PICCADILLY BONGO

JEREMY REED

PICCADILLY BONGO

with a CD of Soho Songs by
Marc Almond

ENITHARMON PRESS

First published in 2010
by Enitharmon Press
26B Caversham Road
London NW5 2DU

www.enitharmon.co.uk

Distributed in the UK by
Central Books
99 Wallis Road
London E9 5LN

Distributed in the USA and Canada
by Dufour Editions Inc.
PO Box 7, Chester Springs
PA 19425, USA

ISBN: 978-1-904634-95-9 (hardback)
ISBN: 978-1-907587-03-0 (signed limited edition)

Enitharmon Press gratefully acknowledges the financial support of
Arts Council England, London.

British Library Cataloguing-in-Publication Data.
A catalogue record for this book is available
from the British Library.

Designed in Albertina by Libanus Press
and printed in England by
Antony Rowe Ltd

CONTENTS

Marc Almond, SOHO SONGS
The CD in *Piccadilly Bongo* contains the following tracks:

Eros and Eye (Almond)
Fun City (Almond/Ball)
Brewer Street Blues (Almond/Neal X)
Seedy Films (Almond/Ball)
Sleaze (Almond)
Twilights and Lowlifes (Almond)
Soho So Long (Almond/Fedorov/Neal X)

MARC ALMOND, vocals
NEAL X, acoustic guitar, harmonica, loops
Recorded at Dean Street Studios

PREFACE TO *SOHO SONGS*

Marc Almond

Soho, such a small part of London, has been a big part of my life as long as I can remember. From stories told to me, books read *(Stand on Me* by Frank Norman), films watched as a kid *(Expresso Bongo, Beat Girl)*, from TV documentaries warning of its dangers for a young teenage boy *(Johnny Go Home)*, it has always been to me a mystical place of red-lit, dark doorways and illicit thrills. It was a universe away from Southport, yet shared some of its seedier secretive sides. It was a natural progression for me to be drawn there and in my late teens I was lured to its streets of promise and shared its sins. I worked there in the late 1970s – clip-joints in Green's Court and Walker's Court, got to know its streets and alleys and became a Johnny that didn't go home. I got to know the ladies at the Golden Girl on Meard Street (and to quote Lady Vivien, none of them were golden and they weren't all girls), wrote and performed cabaret performance shows about it at art college *(Zazou, Dilly Boys, Twilights and Lowlifes* and *Glamour in Squalor)*, and later wrote songs, firstly for Soft Cell on *Non Stop Erotic Cabaret* (its cover featuring the famous shot of Walker's Court) and later for my solo career. Soho continues to be a setting for songs up until now. I lived there on Brewer Street for seven or eight years; I sang and DJ'd and danced in its ever-changing clubs.

Sadly my Soho is disappearing fast. I don't belong there any more and visiting is like going to a foreign land – though I still feel a tingle of excitement walking its streets. Soho is amorphous, as are cities, and Soho is a microcosm, a little city. Each new generation will have their own Soho, hopefully, which will have meaning to them, be a part of their growing and experiencing life, for Soho is still full of vibrant life. Or maybe Soho will be just assimilated into the rest of London and become an affectionate memory in history.

For Stephen and Marco

'*All the great stuff I've ever been thrilled by has an element of falling off the wire. The excitement is that it doesn't. It's somebody taking a Grand Prix corner five miles faster than the corner is meant to be taken.*'

Phil May of the Pretty Things

'*When I was young I needed extreme subject-matter from my paintings. Then as I grew older I began to find my extreme subject-matter in my own life.*'

Francis Bacon

BONA VADA

PICCADILLY BONGO

New to the city's nubby underworld,
circa 1982, I'd bongo
with apprehension outside Boots,
or search the honeycomb of corridors
beneath the street, neither for sale
nor picking up, but polarised

to the Piccadilly glut –
bravura make-up, and so thin
I looked a Giacometti,
my buffed red fingernails glossy
as a black cherry.
Got propositioned all the time

by strangers in the underground,
their strung-out, urgent flip-side up
obliqueness of tactics, part fear,
part desperation, high on risk
and big crowd anonymity.
Met in that way on the stairs down

an address book of blue eyes, palpably
coated in loneliness, like chill
walled on a bottle dug from freeze.
Kept going back, and couldn't break
compulsion all summer, and saw
stand in the ginger light a regular,

sniffing the Soho grid at 6 p.m.;
black glasses, black Gestapo coat,
an ostentatious fugitive
tracking a scent, age overdubbed
by electric aura –
70-50 aggregate?

a man separate by his identity,
I recognised as the louche Grand Guignol
of pigment, the gangsterish, street-wired
Francis Bacon, taking time out
as a quizzical spectator
leaning above the subway gate.

POLARI

You'd hear it on the railings
curved like a black banana
a Dilly dialect
like an uncut diamond –
Bona
vada trade –
spotty rent, he's eighteen,
stem-thin and mean
with bruised attitude
selling for metzas
or a spike in an arm,
the veins rubbed out like disinformation.
He's butch not dolly
an illegal fact
quizzing prospective punters
for the psycho in their look
like a lemon twist in gin.
The omi-polone
(queer in a pink shirt)
prevaricates on the corner
like a Barrier Reef fish
flicking back a fin.
Nishta's the boy's answer
like jutting a verbal elbow
at the man's drawlish offer
peeled off his breath.
An edgy Piccadilly day
with undercover monitoring the crowd –
a decoy in white kaffies –
tubed on white jeans
watching a skinny teen
throwing looks over his shoulder
while selecting a wine gum,
the black before green.

JOHNNY

Comes in the shop, as discontinuous –
no roots, no past, no history,
I see him like projected light
and not biology,
blue faded V-neck, with a tear
shaped like a hippopotamus –

he's there pivoting on black baseball boots
and dodgy, but so courteous
I forget drugs are issue here –
the dealer and the underworld,
the man who's here for the man who's downstairs
heaped under blankets on the floor,

computer on, and books piled high
in columns, for books are his trade,
rare first editions and the Beats –
Burroughs, Kerouac, and if the blue sky's
no limit, Leary on psilocybin,
or whisky bruisers like Scott Fitzgerald

and blow your brains out Ernest Hemingway,
his head wound glutinous as a hacked bull.
Johnny's so displaced, he's not there,
it's Monday or it's Saturday?
his grainy face fibred like the bruised roll
of dirty money I've seen wedged into

his fingers, like his gummy sweat's retrieved
the outmost serial number on his palm.
Denied cash, he'll make do with books –
a signed first, if it peaks at three figures –
a Burroughs *Naked Lunch*: his stringy looks
have all the fascination of the drug

that works its chemistry onto his skin,
coke as clean as white powder, with its rip
of power seated in the brain, its drive
towards an optimal sexual reward,
its downside, paranoia and disdain:
I notice there's a mauve burn on his lip.

He comes back upstairs, from the wrecked basement,
as though he's journeyed from the underworld
at Cecil Court, he's that thin, he's all spine
and talks to me, half deferentially
about my poetry, for it's a drug,
another altered state, a word affair

that's transient, like a chemical, but stays
as words grouped round a singular event.
I keep him talking. He fingers the cash
inside his pocket, surreptitiously,
seems glad to be detained, then checks his phone
and dematerialises in a flash.

THIEVES LIKE US (BABY LOVE)

A trashy compensation – theft –
I meet you on Great Marlborough Street,
post-Liberty, post-Selfridges,
the grandiose faux-mansions that you rob
for kicks, removing building blocks
like bringing down a pyramid
by key-hole surgery.
You do it singing *Baby Love* up high,
as though avoiding eye contact you see
a parallel shape-shifting
shop-lifting reality
where everything is up for grabs
by fine-tuning a subtle frequency.
Your shirt's wet from the chemistry,
sweat glands mixed rawly with a citrus scent,
your pulse like an accelerated train
cooling outside our Coffee Republic,
steel-framed Sonata metal chairs,
your juice the colour of a traffic light
spiked by a stripy drinking straw.
The things you've stolen don't mean nothing now,
deglamorised, pedestrian, useless things,
they've lost their fascination and you pick
with inhibition at your gain,
disinterested, coming down
like loosing altitude – then off again,
still singing *Baby Love*, flicky blond hair
layered and butch for eyes all over town.

SUNGLASSES

The cool look, wide-screen Jackie O
blackouts in a circular frame,
eyewear like a tinted limo,

the car sealed like a mausoleum
flash outside Van Cleef & Arpels
for a laminated icon.

Jimmy Dean used shades as purdah,
thunder-black moodies airbrushing
a masochistic gay chutzpah.

Ray-Bans were a Warhol fetish,
industrial, alien wraparounds
glossy as raindropped nail polish.

They're image-props to attitude,
enigma, iris-free disdain,
staging a Rothko solitude

like Kirk's originals, amber
octagonals graduating to brown
lenses, as retro for an edgy star.

Mystique enhancers, Monroe-wear
to hide the bruises, or pushed up
as celeb pointers in the hair,

they're confirmation of a shift
away from centre, someone moved
into the corners, into foggy drift.

With some it's drugs, desperado
cover for altered states, the light
burning in, punishing as snow.

With others it's like a gated estate,
no point of contact tracking through the street
in aviators to meet a blonde date.

SOHO JOHNNY

Wisteria boas a trajectory –
blue tassels lipping lilac tusks
outside my basement, NW3.
May back again, another year
underwritten like a scar,

you missing and your viral load
at last contact optimal,
HIV and drug-induced psychoses
wiping your system, you offline,
anonymous as the concourse

at Piccadilly Circus underground.
Your poems feed me gritty craft –
two books from a co-operative
signposting your subversive youth,
your cloning fix on a singer

whose bed you shared on Brewer Street.
Tantrums and karaoke scenes,
he threw knives at you in between
diva spectaculars
recording 'Vermin in Ermine'.

You're like a quantum particle
existing simultaneously
in two places – dead or alive
body-bagged in a mortuary,
or living, blasted by your cells.

Your letters scored in orange ink
read like a Burroughs narrative,
a drugs lab pharmacology.

Your poems, two or three winners
don't come better and stick with me

in what I remember when out
city-busy and giving mental space
to deep probe issues, they come up
as comforters, familiar lines
like street names mapping out a place.

BORN TO LOSE

He's books. A tricky underside
to dealing, badged Paul Smith jacket
with a re-sewn interior,

serendipitous, klatchy,
dodgy as the chemical
doing neural tantra

in his limbic circuitry.
Saw him once under the river
in the Blackwall foot tunnel

handcuffed to a carrier
of needles got at Centre Point
as a hygiene freebie

from a parked up white van . . .
Sold me first in Soho cafés
like endgaming genealogies –

giving books a funeral
was his lateral rejoinder
letting go their pull

like dropping out of gravity.
Watched him scalpel a pink millefeuille's
chocolate spinal tendril,

unlid the glazed cover
for increase dopamine.
We'd notched grooves on the same stairs

below Piccadilly
gone looking for a stranger
with the keys to the city,

and talked common folklore
like arcane palare,
he de-bagging a *Querelle* –

a signed Grove Press first,
unwrapped like a tissued gold bar
given covering from dust.

DORIAN GRAY

The blond streaks mussed into his eyes
from a gelled stand-up pompadour
blown to red henna tortoiseshell –
he licked a big cat chromed black
5-litre Jaguar

from Cheyne Walk to the West End
and kept on circling Piccadilly
in a slo-mo Boots orbital,
as though obsessed by an elusive trick –
the tough cutie who got away

that late afternoon, met his smile
in Denman Street, but wouldn't stay,
head thrown back in September rain?
The dashboard's ruby crocodile,
the in-car mincy dance-groove's 'I Feel Love',

a '90s rehab pop-tarted
falsetto by Donna Summer . . .
Two boys hang out under an arch,
drug-wasted little rough rhinestones
they stare at the persistent car,

hoi polloi desperadoes on their patch.
He parks underground. Armani
jacket, black shades ledged in his hair,
Thomas Pink gingham button-down . . .
He's attitude above the stair

scanning the subway exodus,
aware he stands out in the crowd,
his aura like a super-cell's

rotating updraft, arms folded
addressing each emergent face . . .

He'll stay like that disappointed,
ageless as a sugar daddy,
40 something, slim, no tucks,
who started out here and returns
fixed to the memory of a place

he can't let go, the roles reversed,
so he's the hunter, and the prey
must look like him, a little less
spectacular and age faster
and kill him one eventful day.

BILLY SHAKESPEARE IN SOHO

You wouldn't recognize him now;
but this man, nut-brown, triangular eyes,
their reflection roomy as a penthouse
conversion filled with blue skyways,
small (5' 5"?) with pitted acne scars,
cratered epidermal fretwork
like mapping poems on the skin,
dreamy, but speculative, one eye on
rising house prices, the other
on a gay poetry anthology;
black tie-dyed T-shirt, a Westwood jacket
worn as designer over beat-up jeans:
the oval head shaped like an apricot;
the solitary aura like dry ice fanned
lifting a magnum from the freezer.
You wouldn't guess, but the obduracy
was in the hands, the way a poet's work
sometimes resembles carpentry;
his sonnets made like furniture
from knotty syntax – cow's eyes in the grain.
For months I singled out this man
in transit in the street, in bars,
a recreation from downloaded genes
or natural accident?
                                    The deeper I
became convinced, the more he showed,
as though a warp in synchronicity
kept on attracting. He was English to
the taste of bitter drunk on the South Downs,
hoppy, but urban, in Converse sneakers,
taking in the bar with a stare
picking motives from grey matter like flakes
from a fish skeleton. The sonnet man? –

I saw him one day with a boy,
beautiful as hallucinated flesh,
apple-skin 17, but mean,
flattered, resentful, but of course the one
celebrated in packed 14-liners,
blond hair, gold earrings, sulky, diffident,
compelled to live it all over again
Mr W.H. chilling in Soho
beside a window polished by the sun.

WAYS TO WRITE A POEM

Attach yourself to a West End rush hour
tagged to the thunder in its groove
at 5 p.m.: people going under
at Piccadilly Circus, thudding stairs
to fan out through the ticket barriers
and keep the poem tuned in to the trick
of avoiding body contact –
(it does small manoeuvres in its head space),
but observe everything, the winter sky
sparkly as a Chanel boucle jacket
(the imagery starting to crystallize)
the red end of the spectrum sky
dusted violet by carbon emissions:
(the brain only receives light digitally
the poem's always in the dark):
and tweak it with a chocolate boost
(lyric feeds on 80% cocoa)
and gun it phrases of remembered pop
(it needs a rhythm as a hook):
and give it risk by making eye contact
as sexual telepathy
(poetry needs hormonal chutzpah):
and wear a purple jumper (poems like
eccentric individuality):
and hang around on the Regent Street side
where a blond boy's a possibility?
(the form demands a strategy):
and stay there working up its arrival
(the bottom line is oddity):
and know the movement won't come round again
(to risk it all is everything):
and start by writing fragments on the wrist
(the veins are like the underground a dare):
and take its mapping to the Northern Line
and go home pretending you couldn't care.

THINGS I DO

WHAT IS POETRY

The thing I do
while Toyoko
paints her big toe
a Shu Uemura blue.
It's an expensive luxury
for which I'm never paid
a mental superstring theory
I do eating noodles in bed
wondering if her fingernails
are best shocking pink, black or red?
Pete Doherty tells me it's good
to add a fuchsia bud
of crimson blood
into the mix –
call it White Lady or smack.
I feel I write on one side of the world
the reader's on the other,
like the way I call the place I haven't been
Pluto or China.
I hear the moment turn up words
convertible by me
to currency –
Iceland Krona, Indian rupee,
it could be yen, francs or dollars,
none of it legal tender, words
are bankrupt on arrival
from the galaxy.
I'm tax-free from lack of royalties
and Toyoko's aqua toes
are blue as the Hawaiian sea
tickling the beach on a blue cloudless day.

HOW I LIVE

Adding one word to another
like a Soviet constructivist
project
slung over the harbour.
The perma-tanned square-jawed broker
with money-coloured eyes
and boxy Prada
looks at me like I'm Al-Qaeda
for writing poems on the underground,
pulling an image from my head
bright as a Swarovski crystal
on the accelerated rush
between Green Park and Piccadilly
as a systems terrorist.
He keypads a Motorola
as intelligence from his wrist,
grey look turned down at the corners,
spiked-up fatty cholesterol?
I give my line a surge of juice
under the city, as the roar
impacts towards Leicester Square,
if you've got it you can do it –
beam up poetry anywhere,
looking at a grey-eyed broker
and his Boston lawyer's hair
done spiky in Islington.
I continue adding volume
to my lyric in his face,
get off, and I've half the making
of my poem's building blocks
with me in the cooling rain,
dodging puddles as I segue
round them on St Martin's Lane.

James brings the subject in like altitude
elevation of an object from datum
his New York gin fizz euphoric thermal
East 32nd Street
throwing on switches for big players gone
into departures, Creeley, Duncan, Dorn,
Olson who uncapped bourbon reservoirs,
big as a lighthouse, lumbering elephant,
atomized, vacuumed into space,
all of them checked out, no more remembered
than personal number plates in gridlocked
retarded evening traffic burnt
by scorching carbon under cherry-coloured skies.
I don't remember anything I've read,
only pop lyrics – I'm in mid-poem –
he sees my notebook on the shop's red desk
next to a Burroughs *Naked Lunch*
the doctored Ian Sommerville photo
giving him plum tomato-red pupils
an alien reptile exported by the USA.
My writing's simply what I do
to fill in time: I look back on the days
as words, like remembering a rainbow
smudged out by grey skies or a falafel
as neutral aftertaste, no interest
in reading myself or others. James's orange fizz
loses pop and hits a plateau,
then re-climbs, picking out a book he needs,
a stapled, resistant beach-blue pamphlet,
and claims it like a win, while I repeat
no interest in the poem I'll complete
placing it nose-up like a 767
lifting above cloud headed for New York.

DELECTATIONS

Writing a pop lyric
the trick's
to get an impact rhyme
that smooches the palate
like dark
bittersweet chocolate:
'there's a map on my body
it's dark as the Congo
its rivers are tricky
as undergound Soho.'
I do it in bed
my head
full of imaginary hooks
my tongue
spiky with Lapsang Souchong:
'I stand in the corner
with sharp attitude
the crease in my shoulder
cut up like my mood'
I move words around
to find
how they best hang together
in and out of the mind
it's like mixing colour
on a white wall
purple for the bedroom
bright pink for the hall.
'Baby you stood in the rain
the pain in your eyes
building like blue thunder
in the back of the skies.'
I write my way through
the blue

end of blue
piloting heartbreak territory.
'It's cool to feel orange
you're strange Genevieve
I'm leaving you my ashes
to stir with your sleeve.'

TEARJERKER

The hurt comes up like a reprise –
Billie Holiday singing small and low
over a broken-neck red rose
in a rundown hotel room,
dee-dum-dee-dum-dee
do, so
blue.
And me at 4 p.m. each afternoon
the cloud formation doing purple tricks
listen to Billy Fury's heart-stopping voice
dee-dum-dee-dum-dee
do, so blue.
Mostly the pain's backtrack flashback
the scar so deep it's a crater
I can't locate like a Mars probe.
You carved me up, it's true,
dee-dum-dee-dum-dee
do, so
blue.
Billy's voice is the panacea
the healing where the cut resists
recuperation, the tone
irremediably blue:
dee-dum-dee-dum-dee
do, so
blue, so blue.
'In Dreams, Halfway to Paradise'
I have them word by word, each note
filling a space inside my head
that's unconditionally full of you:

dee-dum-dee-dum-dee
do, so
blue,
like Fury's best, the ultimate
soft killing downer 'I'm Lost Without You'.

30 BEDFORD SQUARE
for James Lasdun

Your cluttered office, 30 Bedford Square,
the 1980s like a champagne cork
impacting an abrupt trajectory –
you looking like James Dean, your hair
structured like his, but wavier,
cool with the lived-in flash prerogative
of 25? You were my star-turn editor

who wrote like Nabokov, each line compact
with sighting an optimal metaphor.
You read my drafts in red Silvine notebooks,
the light brokering rhomboids on the floor,
and taught me how completion is the art
of reappraisal, and a poem needs
maintenance, like a fast Jag overhaul.

I'd come in Wednesdays, diesel in the air,
cooking with carbons on Tottenham Court Road,
into an island, Bloomsbury's solid wealth
there like the Woolfs' and waiting to explode . . .
Cape was the Maschler epicentre, wired
to virtuoso fiction by his dare,
his astute entrepreneurial frisson

juiced by panache and overreaching flair . . .
I learnt the little of my art from you
and how immediacy refined by care
fine-tunes a poem's breath, its diaphragm.
Our work complemented each other's trick
of turning sensual imagery into
a visually liberating energy

raying out brightly like a jeweller's star.
I lived on tranquillisers – valium
metabolised to acute addiction,
tubed in from Regent's Park, the underground
riffy with menace in my panicked nerves.
We read Marvell, and his update, Thom Gunn,
and started novels with the same firepower

the cheetah feels in bringing down its prey.
We drank on Dean Street: the French House furore,
hoping we'd smash the club that Burroughs called
Brit Literature, with its thug minders on the door . . .
You left for New York, I went underworld,
L'enfant terrible, drug damaged, crawling through
four years of residual strung-out withdrawal . . .

Today I'm steadier, I feel your pull
attract like gravity in what I write,
sitting out on crumbling back steps, the sun
filmic as glycerine in September,
chasing a poem, the red wine I drink
accelerating chutzpah through my veins,

and go inside to read your new e-mail –
you're out in pristine wilderness with bears,
summer beside a mercury poisoned lake?
you boating through clouds, ruminative, alert
to writing possibilities, and how
visceral trout respond towards nightfall
bulleting flies in the red afterglow,

while I return to brash tobacco plants,
their sweet-scented white flowers, and stay outside
trying to get the intractable right,
polish a phrase for you, as time well spent
attentive to detail, and surrender
to lazy radiance, and work with it,
the slow, amazing honey-coloured light.

THE MAD

All day, I work surrounded by the mad,
the drugged, alcoholic writers
whose book jackets face out or in
like wallpaper
at Red Snapper:
the alphabetically pathologized –
Burroughs' smack dependency,
Brautigan's booze and smiley LSD –
little fish darting eyes through his neurons
the colour of lollipops:
Brion Gysin's majoun, honey and hash,
black hallucinogens:
Paul Bowles trance-floating after tamping kif,
a mushroom of raw exhaled smoke
hanging like a dragon in the bedroom:
Kerouac's miles of empties
extending longer than Route 66,
he drank so much, like Fitzgerald,
Faulkner, Lowry and Hemingway,
squeezing a bottle to their mouths
in enervating slugs,
as though they swallowed on an angry snake.
I live with them under my skin,
Frank O'Hara's red sunrise at breakfast,
vodka and tomato
flaming like a supernova:
Bob Dylan's head-splitting cognac
like a firework in the liver:
they crowd me out like self-reflective mirrors,
my type, my kind,
the same compulsive chemistry,
the same rebellious flameout, shattered love,
the same jump with a burning parachute
towards an explosive bad end.

YES, YOU

You're somewhere in the crowd, anonymous.
In my mind you're a cross between
a doll-eyed Euro-Japanese Manga
and a chiaroscuro portrait photo
by Paolo Roversi.
We neither of us know each other's names
but have a premonition that they'll sound
like matching words in a poem,
resonant like finding out this potted flower's tagged
blue aquilegia.
I burn my sugar looking out for you
to happen accidentally
like the page of a book I'll write one day
and be surprised by what I always knew
had lived in me, but never made it out.
I hunt along St Martin's Lane
eye-surfing the Japanese milieu –
my leopard-print coat exciting curiosity
by its glam ostentation in the crowd.
I'm headed nowhere, but appear busy,
the hope I carry in me like the seed
a bird transplants into a red nasturtium.
Yes, you, you're on my frequency: we hit
some little notes like gold dust in the eyes –
our heads pulled round in reverse symmetry –
two passing strangers in our disappearing act.
I keep on searching, knowing you're out there,
but wide of me, and sense that we'll click soon,
and think too of my aquilegia
open and responsive to the bee's tune.

WHY I HATE POETRY

I prefer Maltesers to poetry,
asymmetrical chocolate moons, they're like
planetary outriders to Saturn or Mars,

crackly ovoids dissolving on the tongue.
I don't know why Brit poetry seems stuck
like a car locked into reverse

churning backwards into the past.
I'm with the present like the newest drug
altering brain chemistry.

Prose does it better. Haruki Murakami.
It gets the detail, like the things girls do
sharing an i-pod or buying paste rings

coloured like marzipan or blue lagoons.
Poetry needs a ritual suicide
a scarlet fry-up like a post-op sunset,

an end that generates a crazy new.
I'm so thin I'd like to leave a window
and touch down in weak gravity

like a re-entry suicide.
The things people do. I once knew a man
fitted a crucifix to a syringe

each time he shot into a vein.
I write to have something fired-up to read
the colour of crushed strawberries.

It's metabolic. So too Maltesers,
and how they communicate sugar hits,
the chocolate slick as a new cricket ball.

I'M LEFT,
YOU'RE RIGHT,
SHE'S GONE

I'M LEFT, YOU'RE RIGHT, SHE'S GONE

A potted full-on red begonia,
frilly as seafood
does its scarlet runway splash,
the detail so hypnotic that it blinds
in bleachy friable July,
more compact than dahlias, brighter

than poppy or anemone
in smudgy silks.
The blonde. I'm left, she's right
in going, no longer rays out
her platinum hair to dry,
a Camel angled in her mouth

at the back door, taciturn, cool,
her mood dark
as a Danish winter or black bark.
Crows mobbed her everywhere
using her as psychic radar,
a sort of central point of gravity

located in her back brain.
She never spoke, just drank French wines
and watched movies in a dark room,
Hitchcock, von Trier, Almadóvar,
and dressed so perfectly in black
Armani or French designers

she always looked a slow-burn star
reading a book, or stepping out
for local DVD rentals.
She never noticed red begonias
explosive as meringue, so red
they seemed lipsticked like Thai hookers

crowding it on by scented pinks.
Mostly she'd play Jacques Brel, Sort Sol,
the downer the better lyrically.
I'd read her poems written off my nerves
dismissively, disparage them
as an addictive failure –

a time-wasting pathology?
I noticed every flower's disruptive show
sitting at her feet on the steps
feeling the concrete hurt my bone,
telling myself expectantly,
'I'm left, you're right, she's gone.'

THE BLUES

There's always someone in the rain –
go ask Alice, Mona,
Jane:
an orange or a red dress on
no money for the train:
the riff comes in and starts to bleed
slide into
inconsolable need
and picks it up again
like stitching a seam.
There's always someone lost it all
down on their knees or up against
the wall,
go ask Alice, Mona,
Jane
to articulate their pain,
a shocking pink or black dress on
no money for their man
no money for the train:
the riff picks up again alert
this time to hurt
and needles the disconsolate
always standing out the rain,
go ask Alice, Mona,
Jane,
dumped and standing there alone
sweat stains mapped under their arms
no credit on their phone,
having a dose of the blues
inconsolably again,
hair roots showing through the dye,
go ask Alice, Mona,
Jane,
why they're standing in the rain?

SAM

Her fringe a hide-behind
for nut-brown eyes:
her shyness like emotional stick-change,
that sensitive, her mood
turned dusty as a peach,
the blue down furring like a foggy day,
Samantha Patrikopolous
doing her global from Melbourne,
walked into my life like a photo-shoot
introspective as blue on blue
or grey in grey
one plateau-flat Soho Friday,
October 8, retarded sunlight;
just one bag and no place to stay,
her nerves glinting like sugar grains.
I gave her my spare key
spontaneously,
no referentials, just instinctual trust
in Sam the teenage journeyer
as right to fill my space with her
blue oceanic generosity.
She stayed three months, reconfigured my shirts,
like ironing confectionery,
a strawberry pink, candy-striped blue and green,
quiet as a cloud shadow, and still
within her movements, like she trapped a thought
on its intangible surface
like polka dots.
When she moved on, she left behind
a Sunsilk deep brunette shampoo,
no other trace of her, its amber leak
staining the bath like a treacle tattoo.

CHIPPED RED TOE POLISH

Degraded gloss
and hers is a Ferrari red,
the top coat flaking to nacreous star-belts
a futures map.
Think Humbert doing brushwork on her toes
in Kubrick's *Lolita*, immaculate
reconstructed strawberry,
like writing a sonnet with dense lacquer
60% Shakespearean ethanol
(formaldehyde free).
These chippy planets, projected right foot
through open-toe sandals have nicked fretwork
(the poem's title's a pop song):
and on the big toe varnish scrolled
like peeling wallpaper, or white membrane
rippling through red snapper scales.
These are her little inconsistencies,
an urban theme, like chemical decay
to be addressed by writing poetry
with Chanel or Max Factor
in a mood like a distracted white stripe
laid horizontal to grey,
on a beachy, open-ended,
resigned to doing nothing cool Sunday?

CHRYSANTHEMUMS

Bitterish, tail-end of October scent,
yellow as tarte au citron, a soft fist
200mm
if you like them big, Chinese outtake,
oogiku in Japanese, a bloom head
saucer-sized, potted on a grave
like a sunburst, or the white,
crisp as a laundered shirt with fifty arms
and a mustard nipple for an eye.
It's a hard word to incorporate in song,
Marc Almond gets it on 'J'arrive',
(I'm coming) in four syllables, each vowel
filled like a chocolate with praline,
an optimal chrysanthemum lament
like stripping a shirt from the back.
Today, I'm sent raffish maroon,
a tangy cluster hubbing pussy willow
and holly tubed into ox-blood red paper,
a friend's gift from Henry & Williams
020 7435 3876,
a tonic, uplifting, emotional churn
of winter blues inherent in their mix,
I hold like a partner against
my turquoise jumper, refreshed by their chilled
seasonal bushiness, tall-stemmed intruders
I'll take into my life choosing
the right black vase shaped like a funeral urn.

JAPANESE CONDOMS

Kimono or Okamoto
airbrushed on they're so translucent,
sensual as a magnolia petal
stained with cerise blusher,
weightless, skinless, 500,
in blue, black or menthol green boxes,
rewrite poetry as rubber
haiku.
      It's the ritual
of unpacking the collapsed oval
(fragile as a contact lens)
the way a catwalk model's
fitted to a sheath backstage,
lyricized skin to skin
immediacy,
          as though I brushed
in passing a poppy's silk skirts
and wasn't sure I'd touched the frill
or made direct contact with light.

MULTITRACK

The memory's brighter than the photograph,
time-framed, undated, but mid-afternoon,
circa pre-AIDS 1980,
he's bony thin, his lover chic,
both dissolved by the stripy light,
one dressed in pink, the other black.

Never let go that instant, can't
forget. I'd've made a stab,
but stayed backgrounded, out of it,
feeling my youth build in the sun
as permanent – the sea right there –
mixing its colours, blues and evergreens.

Later, a furry mist turned strawberry,
the coast fogged-up. I left the beach
in search of two I'd never find,
pretended in a bar I had a friend
who wasn't there – loneliness plays such tricks –
but couldn't turn the absence round.

Today the loss seems multiplied
by all the missing – those who came and went
but stayed permanent on recall,
his legs were runway pins, his friend
a bottle-blond – both obvious –
the sea beating a samba as it turned.

Dead or alive? – there's no tracking
head-turners atomized in memory,
and always there, a Nikon raised
for randomized snapshots – me standing back
out of the picture – wishing now I'd been
up for the moment, wild, reckless and free.

JERSEY BREAKFAST

Three white clouds tailback outside my window,
treetop shaped like oak summits
they're level with. I contradict
their inert vaporous complacency
with my wired anxiety:
too little sleep, the deficit

leaving me fuzzy – a whiteout
abstract as foggy signatures
filling the bay with grainy stuff.
The road I walk to clear my head
is coded in my arteries –
a granite archway, a slab of beech trees,

a sunken farmhouse La Retraite,
buried in its green ecosphere
and managed now by two black Range Rovers
parked up like MOD cars at the gate.
I'm here two weeks each year: the flashbacks seem
hallucinated in intensity,

as though the past's all edited on film
in scarily exact chronology:
bits of my life sequenced as digital
reminders of a ripped documentary . . .
One cloud detaches, and three move on.
The sky tells me the colour of the sea.

Back home I think of breakfast. Cooper's tea,
so smoky it brews autumn in the pot,
a lapsang with such chunky wrigglish leaves
they look like skeins of seaweed on a beach.
Toast's my pretext for Ginger Marmalade,
made by Elvina Davey, 'Burra Tor',

with oranges, lemon juice, ginger root,
from an adapted country recipe:
it spikes the palate without being hot.
These are my ingredients for poetry.
I meet the day full on. The windowed clouds
keep matching form with perfect harmony.

CHOCOLATE MOUSSE

Mahonia outside, whiffy, lemony,
sharp as a tear duct, as you melt
Valrhona

into a druggy espresso,
a black on black vanishing point.
I'm all nose reading Ashbery's

space-time excursions. Dreams are mauve
like the detail you'll add to chocolate,
a single candied violet.

I'm bilocated by the kitchen door
remoting 'Purple Haze', wah-wah
doing sonic UFOs across the floor.

You take a spatula in hand
to beaten egg whites, sugar the mix
to lift like Monroe's cycloned skirt.

I bleed Ashbery into Hendrix,
impure, you say, like mousse backnotes
of raspberry coulis, star anise,

or whiplash lemon verbena.
The light comes inside from so many stars
it lacks a moniker.

I'm for the space olfactory;
you concede cardamom as rogue
invader to sovereign cocoa.

We tipple Vermouth in the wait.
Your mousse sits in French white porcelain
a chocolate muscle in a cup.

POPPY SEED AND CINNAMON PARFAIT

The book I read leaks desert sand –
Paul Bowles' minty cool, his diffident
pathology's Sahara chill,

his stories tamped with kif: blood in the fridge,
who drank it as a desperate rite?
The twist is hoodoo. I soak plot

into my skin like a trout spilling jewels
on slinky opaline.
The stories that I own about myself

and others given a dream-shine
I talk up over lemonade marmalade,
transpersonal stuff like ownerless TV.

Tonight I lift out through the blue
window framing Highgate Wood,
a cube as solid as the fridge

containing poppy seed parfait
the 30ml/2 tablespoons dark rum
tangoing with cinnamon

as a dissolve, a clean friction
the taste buds field, the pestled seeds
scattershot like a blue hail fall.

I zero in on temptation,
the cold prose in my hand solidifies
to watermelon granita,

another option, still unmade.
A green moon's pinlight makes it through
cloud dollops, me just standing there

rehearsing taking out the tin
and cutting a thick slice, the cobalt grains
speckling the knife like caviar.

J.G. BALLARD'S DIET & VIRTUAL FOODIES

I'm vegan. Think anorexic,
ways to metabolize so minimal
I'm like the 7,000 songs
stored on an MP3
in chemistry

or on a chopstick thin
REM lyric
abseiling down the page.
I read Elizabeth David at night
like virtual foodies do,

colour ideas of crisp bruschette,
strawberries botoxed with black pepper,
orange and beetroot jellies.
starry quinoa pilaff,
broccoli macadamia . . .

Neutrinos have three flavours
electron, muon and tau,
subatomic particles.
They pass through matter like the beam
signalling poetry

as what comes through
weightless and
blue.
Ballard does parma ham for lunch
drizzled with truffle oil,

a tyre-shaped omelette à la Shepperton
for dinner, or eat out lobster,
a crab dish, or a shouty steak,

high cholesterol quota of quail
grouse frisked with burgundy ...

It fires his engines for a DJ mix
of prose and omega-3 fats,
the large scotch drunk at 8am
abandoned now – his arteries
clean as a runway at take-off.

A LOVE LIKE YOURS (DON'T COME
KNOCKING EVERY DAY)

A purple sofa, leopard print cushions,
our conversation, Debby
and me,
11 a.m. West End chemistry,
a velvet sleeper sofa (Bloomingdales)
roomy as a re-scripted Cadillac
interior, its ripple like a storm
busy with accelerated electrons
thrashing above the river, indigo
turbulence in the sticky atmosphere?
We talk of book bills, they're like faulty stairs
in a house bombed by insurgents,
the scorch marks signatured across white walls.
Our conversation drifts to sunglasses –
bang on trend futuristic silver frames,
and how the London air's so full
of particles, they seem to pixelate
like free-floaters, nitrogen dioxide, ozone,
sniffy pollutants smelling like seaweed.
We cocktail subjects, a Dumb Blonde shampoo,
vintage repro tail lights, a some day drink
in the neighbouring Beaujolais,
and back to purple sofas, smoochy things
on which to luxuriate, do recreational excess,
with the night outside blackening like a bruise.

YELLOW IRISES

Mustardy splash
with a purple-chocolate coronet
I manage 8
going on 10
if I'm attentive, spiky flash

loud in unrefreshed London soil
coned in a cracked terracotta pot.
Their yellow silks are kimonos
without a sash
split open by data in light.

I tend them assiduously
as co-dependents, scrolling tongues
I feed:
little extensions of myself
I need

to need.
A Boeing's engine rumble roofs
the air with thunder.
We're all so vulnerable
doing our thing with urban green

coaxing a fritillary,
a fragilely bruised
ixia –
names like poems
jumped out of the airwaves

into flower.
Me, I do what I can
with water, own nothing but words

to recreate the pull
I feel

for yellow irises
flourishing on our bashed back steps
this steamy afternoon
of big events and small
insects in tune.

BERETS

They're pancake-shaped, a stylist's wrap
for attitude, not squidgy fill –
spinach/ricotta dreadlocked in a roll.

A Basque motif, worn poppy red
by Carlist purgings, they splashed up in fields
beneath an 1800 corona,

rebellion written in the tilt.
Adapted by virtuosos
the angle batted for the give away –

a glamorous slant to one eye
the dusted up Left Bank intellectual
or the clumpish raised-pie military scoop –

badges pinned to inner cardboard backing.
Kneaded into shape, fisty or flat,
they're nippled, some tie in the back,

others boast fetishy leather sweatbands.
Black's best, and April in the wear,
a fizzy shower rapping over town,

the tempo upbeat, beret kill
an indie cult vocabulary
fusing the arch and practical

in how the wearer moulds the sit
to centre or off-centre crown,
drags hair to a compact shut-out

and signals sassy or macho
or something equally ambiguous
today in rain, with shot clouds blinding by.

SOME PEOPLE

BILL FRANKS

The window open on the river's frog-green tracks
at Albert Embankment, the smudgy tide
licking at Vauxhall – you on the fourth floor –
your closest neighbour, piled up clouds
dispersed like a shattered magnolia,
you dressed in a pristine white polo neck,
always looking towards the other side
for your dead lover? I can feel the rip
the current maintains, its hard shoulder pour
accelerating. You're all equipoise,
the custodian of sixties memories
reactivated for my book. You smoke,
and tell me pain from an eroded disc's
your one argumentative inner dialogue.
John Stephen's partner, you blazed at the core
of fashion mania, saw Carnaby Street
detonate to a pop-starred apogee,
a torrential groove of clothes-obsessed youth.
You fire-up, co-directing the story,
my slight promptings helping initiate
associations that bring the present
into the room as 1963.
I watch you convert black-outs into facts,
remap shop interiors, route orange floors,
arresting drapes – it lasted a decade
the burn-out, the 18-hour working days,
John's manic drinking, his furious designs,
his moment a monumental event,
so packed it seemed his body would explode.
You bring it all alive: the river air
conflicting with the heating's swampish pulse,
the space between us so electrified
it simmers when I flick an outstretched hand.

We ease back to real-time. The winter sun
does takes on the 21st century,
and on a ferry thudding into view,
tourists on deck, the water green and grey
and bluer over towards Waterloo.

RUSSELL HOTEL

The King's Bar. Scarab green armchairs,
your hair so black, it's inkjet black,
and solid like a Niagara
shattering to atomized black,
your poppy red shirt and lipstick

familiar signposts as we sit
three years apart, re-tracking time
from a selective repertoire.
Athens in your eyes. Its white light
so different from the soupy bleed

of October in Russell Square –
orange starfish, or are they leaves?
nosing like planets through the air.
You're here to speak on poetry
and scraped me from a Greek pillar

a sassy Marc Almond poster
shaved from Vouliagmenis Street
October 3, 2003.
Mostly we talk Leonard Cohen,
his matchlessly saturnine songs

saying the lot, without the need
to open an anthology.
Poetry's a retro-virus
auto-destructing on itself
it's got to be that ordinary . . .

We share time here in Bloomsbury,
Virginia Woolf's '20s locale,
and think of her mad in the street
in an egg-streaky négligée,
Leonard shouting after her with a coat . . .

Our friendship's like the Greek mountain
on which you live, that permanent.
We know it's there even in fog.
We have two hours before your train
to bring the summit into view –

a rainbow seems appropriate
like the one that turns visionary
in Cohen's 'So Long Marianne'.
You show me photos. Attikis.
A bronze god signposting your gate.

We keep the window's grainy light,
monochromatic Holborn grey
shot through by polluted sunshine.
We traffic moments together
like diamonds, blue hexagonals

to be reorganized by memory.
Their clusters sparkle. When you go,
camelhair coat collar turned up,
they're in your eyes, bright energies
creating new stars in our galaxy.

MARGARITA

Five minutes late – the little extra pain –
emotional damage and its legacy
holding you back, red Russian hair
bobbed for the breeze to lift, reorganize
to right or left, each way will win
attention for the accidental change?

I sit expecting you in a café –
the Shangrilas romancing on CD:
red chestnut flowers picked to bits by the wind.
I look for your blueblack astrakhan coat,
collar up – you dreaming with eyes open
of Russian forests – once you saw a bear

somersault into strangulated growth,
your heart igniting fast as a BMW's
rip into accelerated drive?
That bear's inside you still as a flashback,
a recreated panic energy.
You come in, untouchably solitary,

bringing the day indoors, gold on your skin.
Your looks turn heads. We group into our own
defensive sharing: it's your marriage took
such breakage, there's scar-tissue on your heart.
You've placed the loss inside a Zen window,
abstracted pain, but the roots come alive

like small fish browsing through a sunken tree
submerged in a green lake. You smoke and draw
on memories of trading precious stones
in India: sapphires and lapis lazuli,
planetary chips blasted out of the stars
to regroup here as mineral glitter.

We talk the world into our radius.
The damage done? I too can't undo hurt,
the sort that breaks a life irremediably.
We shift around it like stroking a blade.
You close your eyes and drop down vertical
into a lift shaft. I stay on alert

and watch you surface. We swim back again
to ordinary compensation like tea,
talk of a book you're reading, Kundera's
death-ethics saturating Immortality,
or of a band that resonates, two-chord
stick-in-the-veins stuff, or arguably three.

Life's like that. Chunks of broken narrative
signposting things we share. You leave at six,
re-zoned across the city, meeting friends,
and when you go I imagine a bear
rumbling the ground, you frozen in your tracks
feeling the atoms tingle in your hair.

JOHNNY DEE (SONGWRITER)

An ankle-length black leather coat
in friable
incandescent July
enough chunky turquoise worn at the throat
to satisfy an Aztec:
turquoise repeated studding a broad belt,
the long post-hippie hair streaked grey
as fox fur.
We spent a summer sharing a table
a skewed three-legged rust-eroded misshapen affair
unbalanced as our minds,
me writing *Dorian*, a novelistic botox
of Wilde's original schizoid longevity theme,
and you still writing songs, your big moment
the Pretty Things' 'Don't Bring Me Down'
charting at No. 3
circa 1965, then covered by Bowie . . .
You nipped whisky into double espressos
and shook like the Hungerford Bridge,
your toke the length of a chopstick
flaking like a dirty firework. Raw grass.
You played me songs that you were demoing,
gritty, lyrical, off the street,
mixing tough social consciousness with jewels
shaped by saliva, emeralds
coated with invective. Your tachycardia
was like stampeding elephants.
You were compassionate, streetwise, displaced
behind dark shades and shot by booze
to paranoid dementia.
We shared a lateral dialogue, a dusty sun
under a striped awning, July to September,
you talking crossfire to my written page,

me drinking Lapsang Souchong, you whiskey
clandestinely: I miss you, generous man,
fine lyricist, and all the bits of you
I can't get down, but always remember.

COLIN

Thirteen steps down and thirteen up,
the basement's shark – curved stairs to the top floor,
he's touching 60, but he's 55,
a dealer with a cockney drawl,
the camp inflected like hair dye
into a heel-cracking masculinity –
he walks always as though treading on glass,
crisp, fast, an abrupt staccato,
hair parted linearly on the left side,
and exact as a central marker-line,
a stormy sky colour that's silver-grey,
complexion up, the eyes on blue-alert,
and oddly snail-like in the way they're set
deep in their oval sockets, all their back
involvement caught up in his look.
He deals in polypharmacy –
he has the lot: coke, crack, smack, valium,
the recreational works, the hard
dependencies, takes speed himself
or gets fried by the shakes. Diminutive,
white fitted shirt, charcoal trousers,
an iffy sexuality, that's gay,
if you observe the way his eyes and wrist
co-ordinate as dramatic subtext
to action gestures. Don't know his surname,
or where he lives, only he delivers
with max efficiency: Thirteen steps down
and thirteen up, cashmere jumper tied round the waist,
gives me the count, and sings as he goes out,
'Love Me or Leave Me', and heads into town.

STEELY DAN
for Aaron

Messrs Becker and Fagen
a.k.a. Steely Dan
vocal inflections homegrown like a tomato
in Laurel Canyon,
harmonically narcotic
as melatonin to alpha-rhythms,
their songs are polished like a gangster's
patent leather shoes,
all the drug allusions
dashboard-pocketed
like foils inside the lyrics
that seem to chapter sunny altered states,
sitting out in a dust-filled universe
running an index finger
over blue fuzz on a peach.
They drove respectively
a swank red 1966 Chevelle
and a Nasa silver Mazda
RX-7 econosportsedan,
gunning into the studio
across the international date-line,
that late, arriving Tuesday afternoon
having left on Wednesday
the future having got reversed
in a parallel time-space.
Penniless, disillusioned:
(purple valium are for veterinary
surgeons):
the music shimmered like September light
radiant with gold dust
slanting on the moment

of 'Any Major Dude':
Messrs Becker and Fagen
their songs are like prescriptions
I can't do without,
they're a language in my genes,
an upbeat, ripe-orange postscript
to my moody disaffected teens.

MEETING EDMUND WHITE

Autumn's mushed leaves were flatfish-specked drift,
October bottled like claret,
you museumed all day at the BL,

researching insects 1823
for a new novel, me in a café
scribbling to orangey anodyne pop,

the afternoon advancing, black by four,
me jump-starting the journey across town,
jittery, 20 years of reading you

assimilated, your novels composite
in me like building blocks,
molecular subterranea.

Me early, you in a green winter coat,
sandily youthful, ex-YSL chic,
purposefully dressed for the London winter,

your genial spontaneity
so roomy, we were friends becoming friends
who'd waited on that moment.

Later, the hotel bar, we Francophiles
talking up Genet, Proust, then tearjerkers –
John Wieners and Jimmy Schuyler,

consummate, broken-hearted lyricists,
madness the rogue cell in their poetry.
I watched experience written up in you,

the good shot through by the endemic plague,
and you its elegist, re-writing loss,
turning compassion on it like a sun.

We parted by the fast-laned Euston Road,
both turning round, flashed by the sudden cold,
hands raised, then overtaken by the crowd.

HELIOGABALUS

Faggy in a tiara
he watches the foggy river
hair bleached with henna
he looks like Lou Reed circa
1974
watching the iffy Tiber
make tracks to the shore.
Black shades, black biker boots,
he sniffs at the docks
Invictus Sacerdos Dei Soli
cruising the bath houses,
patron saint of rent.
A drowned boy's puddled
under a wharf,
he pulls him out head first
one of the lost
reclaimed by mother,
then kicked back in the tide.
It's AD 218
the chilled fog at his throat,
he stands collar up
on a floor-length leopardskin coat,
Dei Invictus Solis Elagabili
bottle in his hand,
boots mapping incunabula
on the muddy sand.
He's a butch faggot
selling attitude,
hearing a ferry broker
a wailing course downriver,
its wake sloshing froth
over a pointed boot.
He's scared of the soldiers

carving him up
an emperor in drag
couched under the piers,
startled by the foghorn
miked into the soup
and by a snouty rat
sizing up his foot.

JACK THE RIPPER

A lipsticked Ali Baba
Victorian
Michael Jackson wannabe
hanging out in fishy alleys
vacuum-sealed with fog
smoky blue and sepia
furring Whitechapel's
piss-tangy corridors,
he hung out solo
folded into a badged coat
a sexy tattoo
inked on his throat.
Lived on a house boat
with a music hall singer –
all legs and mascara
and rudimentary cockney
brash as lemon zinger,
lippy and punk
in a paste tiara.
Nights that he didn't come back
she had a girl lover –
Marge from up near Wapping
selling sex by the river,
but butch in a man's shirt
and strappy red braces.
When he came back drugged
and with a furred tongue,
there were blood stains on his shirt
that she made into a song,
called it the Ripper,
it tore up her life,
red as the exit sign
delivered by a knife.

LISA'S

Arroyo Grande,
each word shaped like a red love heart
from a triangular
matt Mac Russian Red lipstick mouth
a hot strawberry
celled in my ear.
Mileage Chart: Los Angeles 185,
Monterey/Carmel 153,
San Luis Obispo
15,
her glow
diffusing through me as bright energies,
stars coming on, the Pacific
behind her beached in her spine
65.3 million square miles of impacted momentum
atomized in her voice
that settles in my ear
with tingly sparkle.
Lisa's beret's black
as seaweed, black
as underwear,
her personality scintillating
as emotional jewellery.
Love on a cell phone: Californian fog
blowing its smoky architecture round her head,
turning the sun to blue neon,
her purple car parked within easy reach
of where she's sitting with her cell
talking to me on a surf-hissy beach.

IAN

Drops in, cold molecularized in his hair
from planet Burroughs (editing)
the green-skinned
cyber gun-toting alien reptilian's
dopamine-flushed personal letters.
The day's twinkly January aquamarine –
clouds forming a dyslexic alphabet
over the National Gallery's
cryo-frozen art mortuary:
a place I visit for pop star postcards –
the Rolling Stones by Gerard Mankowitz,
circa *Aftermath*, 1965,
a black-and-white moment locked into time.
Ian's silk paisley scarf's like poetry –
turquoise and red Indian bodhi tree leaf motifs
microscopic paramecia,
half yin yang symbol patterned on gold,
the detail coded full-on in my need
to work the impact into imagery.
Burroughs looked part vulture, part mortician,
zero-size in designer suits,
a cool forensic drugs-lab in a tie
the colour of a runway, nerves cooking
analgesics from a needle and spoon.
We talk him up as chemical hero
accelerating prose like rocket fuel,
and talk him down to death factors,
quadruple bypass, an open casket,
the thin man laid to rest in a black suit
splashed with red roses, a gun in his hand
at Liberty Hall in Lawrence
one sweaty Kansas August afternoon.
We huddle by the one heater, fired up

by projects, possibilities, and watch
hexagonal snowflakes dust eyelashes
on the street window, catch our breath
as atomized glitter, and look out hard
at crystallized fonts, take a whisky slug
and burn with its exhilarating roar.

A BIGGER BANG

A BIGGER BANG

The river's unstoppable flow
a guitar-driven
green-skinned Nile or Congo,
the riffs on it co-extensive with time,
the Stones on the road
like reading global blood-pressure
an ECG read-out
of catastrophic apocalypse
the road that only goes one way
to accelerated liquidation,
burning towers, corporate giants
evacuating cities in their jeeps
under a dragon-shaped smoke cloud
chasing their shoulder.
The band's the epic
soundtrack
amped-up anaesthetic
for final things – the President
crashing into his swimming pool
torched by a bomber in his suite,
his suit finned by red flames.
The road churns on –
their thunder roofing stadiums
1.5 million an hour
dollar bravura
virtuoso circuitry –
a Jagger, Richards, Woods, Watts, turbo-thrust
at making out with history
in buckskin boots and edgy coats –
a plutocratic rock circus
working the edge – it still goes on,
power as it's driven right to the stage hem
like an electrocuting hurricane.

WHY THE ROLLING STONES ARE SO SKINNY

A neuroendocrine deficiency?
from circa 1963,
same body weight, same lasered to the bones
skinny confederacy:
average 63.5 kilograms
(140 pounds) topped by canned Guinness
as a black iron-compounded supplement
tasting of fermented Liffy.
Is it the light-speeding riffs keep them thin,
Chicago blues given amphetamine
guitar figures, or weird vasopressin
piloting the brain's chemistry?
Jagger's all carbohydrates: pasta, rice,
wholemeal bread, sushi for protein,
Richards and Woods spar cigarettes like chords,
nicotine-fencing and chase 'Nuclear' vodkas
slashed into orange (quadruples)
into liver toxicity,
streamlined defiance of all body laws,
a Stones individuated chemistry,
teeny bodies with reptilian pigment
like snakeskin grafted to anatomy.
Dysfunctional hypothalamus?
drugs or a Ferrari-charged stage anxiety,
they're wiry as contorted poppy stems
twisting their necks into dusty blue flower.
Their statement's irreversibly maintained,
skinnyness as salutary
the body copied like a guitar neck
and belted into max 30" jeans.
The riff for 'Jumping Jack Flash' strips off flesh
like meltdown, it's an aviation thrust
that shuts time down for the song's duration,
the licks so volatile, they're played on nerves
blasting a g-force assault on all calories.

SWAMP BLUES

A liver-toxic, muggy swamplands mix –
the Stones surfacing like alligators
to brew voodoo
soupy riffs in the studio.
Knobbled sexagenarian virtuosos

on skewed legs
socketed into chinos,
their sound's like ripped dark energy
accelerating from cosmic Big Bang
across a radiated universe,

mashed, sticky with its greenhouse scars
and manipulative oil wars.
They're like four figures turning gold
in a bunker urinal
a declassified rock hegemony,

no charts, just live
conquistadorial rock,
a global liquidation act,
extravagant funeral rites, light the fat
and keep on playing in the frying pan's

electrifying drizzle.
'Rough Justice' turns up like a bailiff's threat
throwing punches on the door.
A gritty street edge still skins their fingers
bleeding from abrasive chords

like stripping fish.
It's late, murky, a riffy cosh
of affirmative attitude

that they're invincible – bandit rockers,
skins printed out as dollars, cash,

wonky hats and leopard-print coats,
parading leather-baked longevity, dried out,
detoxed, gangsterish autocrats,
turning the volume up like overdose
or blow-out in a nose-up lifting jet.

IN MY TIME

IN MY TIME

Keith Richards snorts his father's ashes with cocaine
as make-up for the mind, a freebased dirt,
cocaine hydrochloride
doing its faster than light front brain thing.
Somebody's funeral kebab in Iraq's
bitty with human gristle, visceral offal,
whisky bottles placed on a burnt-out tank,
a Jack Daniels spiked with a scarlet rose
red as a valentine heart, lipstick red.
And me, buying an organic broccoli
to boost my anti-oxidant war with free radicals
are out choosing a John Smedley jumper,
peppermint green with candy stripes
so pastel cool it's ice cream lickable.
Whatever's seen is dated by its time,
our moment coded with a sell-by date
like blueberry yoghurt, or an airticket
to somewhere dodgy like Dubai.
My unstoppable thoughts repeat themselves
then loop into a black hole, and nosedive
into the final dark. It's happening now,
whatever's in the air and in my cells,
another day burnt into deletion,
remembered by a Red Snapper book launch –
Pete Doherty signing in scarlet nail polish,
the rain outside, unrepeatable rain,
in snappy showers, and I'm in Cecil Court,
writing this poem, Whitehall down the road
guarded for war crimes like a bunkered fort.

ATIVAN

A benzo
blunt heart-shaped sublingual
beach-blue tablet
used to feed me every day
the addict's chilly slow-hit glow
the ritual popping of the foil

a tear like a carjack
ripping a silver-painted door:
the blue got from indigo carmine,
E132; a studied hit
that levelled like I'd made the floor
a flight above from one below

without a power surge.
I kept a foil in each pocket
like a drug quango
kept them for emergency
like a bunkered czar
in a post-junta round up,

the stuff I knew tracking
my GABA receptors
unmasking jitterbug paranoia
big as a rock stadium.
I got scripted by an offshore doctor
a sort of George Nichopolous

prescribing Elvis Presley
Dilaudid, Quaalude, Dexedrine
in repeat hundreds.
I kept the boxes in a vault –
a raft in my shirt drawer
sensitive as fingerprint data,

my user's pharmacological hoard;
stockpiling granular weaponry
against myself, and underground,
compacted on the tube keeping
a tablet clamshelled in my sweaty palm
for fear of stoppage, a boiling blackout

on the blocked Northern Line.
I suffered memory blanks,
amnesic pockets, whiteout fogs,
dependency that brought me to the floor
kicking it, but still keep a box
pharmacy labelled that I can't let go

as a benzo memento,
the loss proportionate to gain? –
but still the need comes up as a small grief
for disinhibited habit,
the user's secret act of swallowing
I felt like a dodgy complacent thief.

THE THIN MAN SINGS BALLADS
for Stephen Andrews

You gunned our Saab's proficiency
across the Westway flyover's
hard shoulder – its post-human fins
skylined above rogue interzones,
en route to Hammersmith Broadway,
old retro highrise blotched like stone-washed jeans

mirroring a jet liner
from their defunctive state of the arts decks
over W6.
You drove into a diffused sun
red as a scuttled Coke can
winged into slipstream,

headed for the hallowed Lyric
and Peter Hammill's first-night trek
through stripped hormonal ballads:
told me on the way his gutsy
virtuoso marathons
were like vocal costume changes

cross-cutting between honey
and cacophony;.
Inside the plush was ketchup red,
the Steinway like a black sarcophagus,
the thin man thinner than a drinking straw
sat at the piano,

impassioned, colouring retreads
with agonised fortissimo,
hands boning chords,
voice somatizing 20 years

of cutting edge with poignancy,
emotion raw as chopped onion;

the tension stacked like thunder
rolling in a miked-up sky,
the thin man banging crescendos,
no resolution to his oomph,
his blue moods going indigo,
his power like an Al-Qaeda sting.

We pointed the car back due North,
baseball-bat shaped drops of rain
arriving, and spoke of belief,
unnerved conviction, and how it sustains
someone a lifetime – Hammill's art –
and upped the question burning the fast lane.

ALIEN

Her red hair flurried out of inkjet black,
Asian concession to Euro,
she reads a Lonely Planet Guide,
me studying her hair like botany,
looking for a name for a cute poppy,
rogue outtake
of papaver orientale,
the dark blue poppy here turned black and red
as cultural alien in this bar.
I try to turn her downturned head
by concentrating on her hard
in ray-gun bursts of projected telepathy.
At five I turned adverse to fact,
argued I wanted purple, not blue eyes,
and an alternative biology,
and internalised it imaginatively,
and stayed odd, off-centre and parallel.
I can't tell her my proto-history
of weird personal angles, but watch her scan
her guide that closely, it's another world
she interprets, extraterrestrial,
displaced, as though on an asteroid-belt.
She's a futurian with a pink smoothie
on planet London, boots and mini-skirt,
scrolling her phone, while I plan cheapest flights
lifting me to the far edge of the world.

PETE

Brings me a purple-wrapped Quality Street,
a Jumbo-sized sticky toffee bullet
size of an elongated snail
stretched to max elasticity:
uncaps a bottle of Jack Daniels
as liquid explosive, red fingernails
chipped like the scales from red mullet,
a banjo in a crocodile-green case
slung on the floor like a zoo exhibit.
We talk of poetry, his/mine,
and how beauty if it impacts as real
needs a grit coating picked up from the street?
The space between us moves like fish
nosing undulating serenity.
He shows me notes written at Pentonville,
his loose-leaf prison diary, and blood-art,
disposable syringes blood-coated
with Doherty antigens from O type.
These are deposits in his doctor's bag
of tricks and rehab prescriptions? We nip
the bottle's raw volatile scorching kick,
before he jams with Aaron, prods the Kinks
'Tired of Waiting' into a river drawl,
a Londoner's subsurface dodgy tone,
as though he sang it tilting down wet stairs.
The afternoon breaks up. He segues out,
elusive as a figure cut from rain,
talking of Brick Lane, book-thefts, proto-punk,
aversion implants, and how cherry stones
live in good songs, the hard inside the soft
for durability, and at a run
licks off, black hat skewed, towards Leicester Square.

ODD

Odd that I want to know
the label in a Frank O'Hara shirt
        that's rubbed out dusty blue denim
15" collar casual button-down
        worn as a tight fit on hurt
at 791 Broadway – a floor-through loft
        a big Mike Goldberg on one wall
his resourceful reservoir of deep gossip
        injected into poetry
like Strega poured out slippery on the floor
        because the bottle didn't fit the glass.
The shirt's a Brooks Brothers from Bloomingdales?
        or possibly an Arrow?
not eye candy, but gay-themed leisurewear
        worn in that way, the cut achieved
by pelvic and waist angles, fingers slid
        onto a broad leather belt
as naturally sexy. Odd that I attach
        to detail like a thread
a jacket button, grow obsessed
        by labels, image-minutiae,
the look that spells out attitude
        in clothes and poetry,
and Frank O'Hara's shirt's my grab today
        at quizzing the significant
incidental, a button popped or lost
        included, and the label, shop
important as the packaging and cost?

PRIMARIES

Green written in red
dusted like eyeshadow
smudged on the pavement's grid,
red like a two-door 1969 Dodge,
a graffito's insignia
hot as paprika
chalked up pre-rain –
me out buying *Record Collector*
tracking a schizophrene's rewrite
of colour vocabulary?
Rimbaud's delusional vowels
coded synaesthesia,
A black, E white etc;
but further on the gradient
mauve written in yellow
bright as laburnum tassels,
me scanning a Velvet Underground bootleg
in the Robert Quine series,
drawn to the attached skull
off-yellow like a penguin's cheeks,
the hieroglyph a window
on rudimentary death.
Orange transposed to blue,
Rimbaud's colour for O,
a blue like ceanothus
only jazzier,
an Adriatic ultramarine,
an arrow stemming from the word
towards a blue front door?
I walked on, buzzy with neighbourhood clues,
riffling through Greats and General
my eye drawn to 'Itchycoo Park'
EP France PS Columbia –
open to offers; please call.

LIGHT ON YOU

Dana and Sophie, loaded with muffins,
a Starbucks' sticky blueberry,
bounce in the shop with New York energies
like light arriving from the galaxy –
the 100 billion wobbly stars
with dust compacted in their chemistries
and amazingly talk up off the wall
rubber-expansive poetry.
Our barriers are condom-thin,
swirly and soluble. The things we say
metabolize like Vitamin C.
We're on a star with methane, ozone, oxygen,
supportive gases, but it's burning out
for lack of regenerative overhaul.
It's Friday, fat muffins reduced to paste
for carbohydrates. We play tricks on words
by going silent, letting meaning flick
a white mouse tail out of the shop.
We come back to real matter, that it's cold,
unseasonably so for prime-time May,
and issues like Dana's ten rescue cats
looked after in New York by her mother,
as feline pamperer, and how today
in our location, Bloomsbury, tulips
are winegum-coloured and London's on hold
with terrorist reprisals underground,
no safety in our little group waiting
on fault-lines like stitches sewn in our skin.

LONDON BURN-OUT

The rev accelerates inside my nerves
like a Ferrari Modena Stradale
hot off the blocks: the West End crowding on
into the viscera: impacting smash
of energies, it burns me from the feet
upwards into a dull backbrain headache

unkillable by Aspirin: a flare-up
and I'm skewed off balance for half the day
shot in the head by a neural bullet.
My hand shakes, waiting for Tokoyo's text,
an indicator I'm in someone's thought,
concentrated as a poppy's black eye.

It's 1984 in 2008,
the thought police monitoring every move,
the führer and his suited thugs alert
that Whitehall's the epicentre of threat,
the PM's henchmen helping him into
a bullet-proof vest underneath this shirt.

Everywhere, speed and terror, guns and coke,
the vulnerable and rappy power-brokers,
the slickers with gold fillings eaten up
by money markets. The financial roar,
like a digital lion lashed its cubs
and herded them into a raging fire.

I look for refuge, orbiting its core,
a corner in an under-the-street bar,
a café, or a friend's scrambled bookshop,
or sharing migration to inner space
with those space-hopping to the interior
as a safe precinct from perpetual war.

The city burns on, and my headache glows
backbrain, like lights in an aquarium tank.
A yellow-jacketed paramedic
bikes through the traffic on a warped segue,
stops off to ask directions, then arrows
into a side street as a spiral trick.

I try to hold my own, speed-read the crowds,
and look for light inside a stranger's eyes,
a slow-burn trust, defiant persistence
in human good – sometimes it's one in five
maintain something I see turning to gold,
resistant, pure and vitally alive.

OUTLAW POETS

The further out from centre like space junk
      littering in graveyard orbits,
the more defiant chutzpah. I can hear
      the graffito surge in Marlowe
slashing his inspiration at a wall
      after biting a sailor's ear
in foggy lowlife St Giles with a bear
      escaped cage and sniffing Soho,
or blank Sid Vicious self-harming with words –
      'the mix of personalities
is the critical fing wif a band, now, innit?'
      A smoothie laced with methedrin
might be a tropically coloured intro
      into the poem's hologram
situated like a 3D tomato
      in hippocampus traffic.
Shakespeare preferred brokering real estate
      to writing solid ink sonnets
at the kitchen table, tryptothan
      like a chemical skyscraper
in his muesli supplemented brain:
      black hash in his tobacco pouch,
the 16th-century sunlight coloured red
      like beat-up strawberries.
Poets should be like HIV carriers
      to society, undercover
agents spraying vision across the walls
      of corporate giants, outlaws
turning up words like purple neons,
      and caring nothing for their finds
but how they get an image into orbit
      first low, then higher out of sight
like space junk turning over in the dark
      and at re-entry, burning into light

WHEN THE LIGHTS GO OUT

Jad's treadmill workout triggers endorphins.
Jacuzzi and a black masseur
under the city's nuclear corridors.
Viagra for gonadal aristos
he watches a film of Posh being fucked

by a crocodile of rappers
positioned backseat in a Cadillac's
customized leopard-skin interior.
The fingers groove in his meridians,
release spinal space stations up his back.

He's part of Ruag Munition sales-floor,
the Modular explosive penetrator
his selling point – punchy warhead
adapted to shoulder-fired
anti-tank systems, ripping through concrete

to blast a reinforced bunker.
His DB9's bonded aluminium frame
is coloured silver.   Nosing up the ramp,
the cabin's intergalactic hyperdrive jump
is like a Dorchester honeymoon suite

moulding him to centre console.
His gratis copy of the DVD
secure in a dossier, he disappears
somewhere oily underneath Eaton Square.
He checks the video signal in his hair.

He finds Hans waiting in a Jaguar.
Tonight the Stones play Docklands, the last night
as an apocalyptic finale

to unplugging the planet, fuses blown
on a scorching, amped-up 'Jumping Jack Flash'.

Jad's Mapam mortar's 'superior lethality'
for the assassin facing centre stage.
Hans buys for salvation. He knows the plot,
the darkness at the end of things, the kill.
Jad's tongue is in his mouth and very hot.